The Thirteen Colonies

# Virginia

**Books in the Thirteen Colonies series include:**

# The Thirteen Colonies

# Virginia

Karen Price Hossell

Lucent Books, Inc.
10911 Technology Place, San Diego, California 92127

Library of Congress Cataloging-in-Publication Data

Hossell, Karen Price.
  Virginia / by Karen Price Hossell.
    p. cm. — (The thirteen colonies)
Includes bibliographical references and index.
Summary: A history of the colony of Virginia, which originally
offered the opportunity to escape England's class system and poor
economy but quickly developed its own social strata.
  ISBN 1-56006-995-3 (alk. paper)
  1. Virginia—History—Colonial period, ca. 1600–1775—Juvenile
literature. 2. Virginia—History—1775–1865—Juvenile literature.
[1. Virginia—History—Colonial period, ca. 1600–1775. 2.
Virginia—History—1775–1865.] I. Title. II. Thirteen colonies
(Lucent Books)
  F229 .H79 2002
  975.5'02—dc21

2001002793

# Contents

# Foreword

T he story of the thirteen English colonies that became the United States of America is one of startling diversity, conflict, and cultural evolution. Today, it is easy to assume that the colonists were of one mind when fighting for independence from England and afterward when the national government was created. However, the American colonies had to overcome a vast reservoir of distrust rooted in the broad geographical, economic, and social differences that separated them. Even the size of the colonies contributed to the conflict; the smaller states feared domination by the larger ones.

These sectional differences stemmed from the colonies' earliest days. The northern colonies were more populous and their economies were more diverse, being based on both agriculture and manufacturing. The southern colonies, however, were dependent on agriculture—in most cases, the export of only one or two staple crops. These economic differences led to disagreements over things such as the trade embargo the Continental Congress imposed against England during the war. The southern colonies wanted their staple crops to be exempt from the embargo because their economies would have collapsed if they could not trade with England, which in some cases was the sole importer. A compromise was eventually made and the southern colonies were allowed to keep trading some exports.

In addition to clashing over economic issues, often the colonies did not see eye to eye on basic political philosophy. For example, Connecticut leaders held that education was the route to greater political liberty, believing that knowledgeable citizens would not allow themselves to be stripped of basic freedoms and rights. South Carolinians, on the other hand, thought that the protection of personal property and economic independence was the basic foundation of freedom. In light of such profound differences it is amazing that the colonies were able to unite in the fight for independence and then later under a strong national government.

Why, then, did the colonies unite? When the Revolutionary War began the colonies set aside their differences and banded together because they shared a common goal—gaining political freedom from what they considered a tyrannical monarchy—that could be more easily attained if they cooperated with each other. However, after the war ended, the states abandoned unity and once again pursued sectional interests, functioning as little nations in a weak confederacy. The congress of this confederacy, which was bound by the Articles of Confederation, had virtually no authority over the individual states. Much bickering ensued— the individual states refused to pay their war debts to the national government, the nation was sinking further into an economic depression, and there was nothing the national government could do. Political leaders realized that the nation was in jeopardy of falling apart. They were also aware that European nations such as England, France, and Spain were all watching the new country, ready to conquer it at the first opportunity. Thus the states came together at the Constitutional Convention in order to create a system of government that would be both strong enough to protect them from invasion and yet nonthreatening to state interests and individual liberties.

The Thirteen Colonies series affords the reader a thorough understanding of how the development of the individual colonies helped create the United States. The series examines the early history of each colony's geographical region, the founding and first years of each colony, daily life in the colonies, and each colony's role in the American Revolution. Emphasis is given to the political, economic, and social uniqueness of each colony. Both primary and secondary quotes enliven the text, and sidebars highlight personalities, legends, and personal stories. Each volume ends with a chapter on how the colony dealt with changes after the war and its role in developing the U.S. Constitution and the new nation. Together, the books in this series convey a remarkable story—how thirteen fiercely independent colonies came together in an unprecedented political experiment that not only succeeded, but endures to this day.

## Introduction

# A Land of Opportunity

U nlike many of those who settled America's original thirteen colonies, Virginia's first European settlers were not looking for religious freedom. They were searching instead for opportunity and financial gain. They were Englishmen who were dissatisfied with their lot in life back home, searching for a way to break out of England's class system. Or they were adventurers, weary of the calm pace of life at home in England.

The first settlers were sent to the new colony to find gold or silver or copper. Expecting to get rich quick and return to England with coffers of money, they built tiny shacks, barely large enough for one man to stretch out and sleep in. Then they spent weeks digging for precious metals. When they found none, their sponsor, the Virginia Company of London, instructed them to make silk and wine, but those projects, too, failed. Some gave up and went home discouraged and disillusioned. Many more—nearly 80 percent—died of disease and starvation barely having arrived in the new colony.

Then one settler planted tobacco seeds, and the successful cash crop changed everything. Men who struggled in their lower- or middle-class existence back in England saw real opportunity in Virginia. Many came as indentured servants, unable to afford even to pay their own passage and bound to years of servitude in Virginia. But most of them welcomed the opportunity. They would have nothing like it back home. They worked off their terms, were rewarded with plots of land, and planted tobacco. And some of them indeed became very wealthy.

## A Colony Much Like Home

While Virginia originated as a land of opportunity for those hoping to escape the stuffy class system and waning economy of England, oddly enough, once the colonists made their money in the new colony, they developed a society much like the one they had escaped. They established a state church, the same one in which they worshiped in England. Landowners made the laws and ruled the land, just as they did in England. And, perhaps inevitably, the rich in Virginia got richer through the efforts of the poor and helpless, just as things had been done in England for centuries. Only the institution of slavery distinguished Virginian society from the mother country. The lower to middle class endured for a while; ultimately, though, its members found themselves in a power struggle with wealthy planters who controlled the government and the economy.

The first settlers of Virginia hoped they would have better opportunities than found in England.

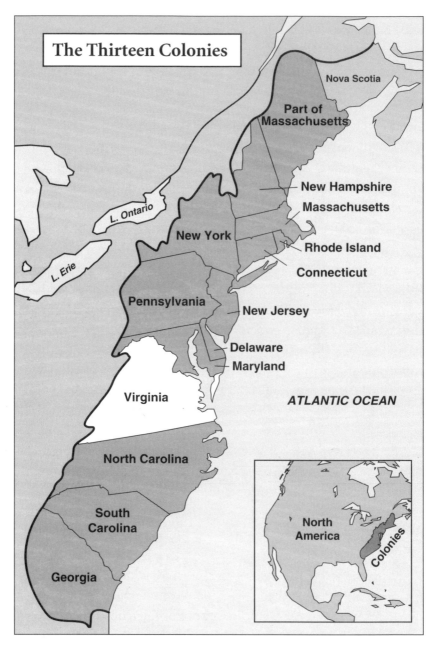

Then revolution changed the landscape and social structure of Virginia. Not until the Civil War did social equality become reality. Virginia went from a land of unlimited possibility to a land of special interests, then back again. The story of Virginia is one worth telling because it reflects the hopes and values of all of America.

## Chapter One

# The First Colony

In 1604 a group of English merchants and knights formed a company whose goal was to establish a colony in the uncharted New World lands called America. The group petitioned King James I, seeking his consent to colonize a large area of land known as Virginia, claimed for England by British explorer Sir Walter Raleigh in the late 1500s. In 1606 King James granted the company—the Virginia Company of London—permission to establish a colony, which he called "the First Colonie," and drafted a charter that proclaimed the goals of the enterprise. One goal was to find a northwest passage to the Pacific Ocean; discovery of an alternative, shorter water route to Asia would be a huge advantage for English traders seeking spices and silk for the European market. Another goal was to find gold, silver, copper, and other minerals in Virginia and ship them back to England. The third major goal was to convert the native American Indians, viewed as savages, to Christianity. The charter stated:

> Hereafter tende to the glorie of His Divine Majestie in propagating of Christian religion to suche people as yet live in darkenesse and miserable ignorance of the true knowledge and worshippe of God and may in tyme bring the infidels and savages living in those parts to humane civilitie and to a setled and quiet governmente. [1]

With these goals in mind, the Virginia Company acquired and outfitted three ships, which set sail from Blackwell, England, on

The Virginia Company of London was granted permission to establish the first English colony in the New World.

December 19, 1606. On board were about 130 men from all walks of life. Many of the colonists were English gentlemen looking for adventure and hoping to make money by exploiting the resources in Virginia. The remainder were selected because their skills were considered essential for the establishment of a settlement. They included carpenters, laborers, bricklayers, a blacksmith, a mason, a tailor, a sailmaker, and a drummer. While the English gentlemen were members of the Virginia Company and had invested substantial money in the expedition, these working men were instead investing time and labor—seven years' worth. They were promised a plot of land in Virginia after they had served their seven-year term of indenture.

The ships reached the Chesapeake Bay and coastal Virginia in April 1607. The commander of the sea journey, Captain Christopher Newport, sailed up the southernmost of the five rivers that flowed into the bay. He found a small harbor and sailed into it, and a few settlers rowed away from the ship to explore the south shore. They were attacked by five Indians almost immediately, and two of the English men were badly wounded. The ships gathered up the injured men and veered toward the north shore. Fifty-seven miles upriver, they found a small peninsula on the north shore and chose that site for their settlement. They readied themselves to work toward fulfilling the colony's stated goals. But instead of discovering a passage to the Pacific Ocean and filling England's royal treasury with gold and silver, the men who arrived in Virginia would spend most of their time and energy struggling just to stay alive.

## The First Months

Before the ships left England, the Virginia Company had selected a council to rule the new settlement. Without announcing their choices, the Virginia Company put the names of the council members in a locked box and delivered the box into Newport's custody, instructing him to open it only after the settlement site was chosen. After the box was opened and the contents revealed, the new council members voted Edward Wingfield as president. They also voted to call the settlement Jamestown, after the king, and they christened the river they had sailed into the James. Then they began to draw up plans for a fort. Meanwhile, the settlers set about preparing the land. Some cut down trees and used them to make clapboards to send back to England. Other settlers planted gardens and readied nets for fishing.

Captain Christopher Newport commanded the ships that traveled to Virginia.

# The Powhatan

In 1607 about thirty large groups of Indians lived on the coastal plains adjacent to the Chesapeake Bay. They were led by a paramount chief, or *mamanatowick*, whose name was Powhatan, and their entire confederacy is commonly called by that name.

Each member of the Powhatan confederacy worked to ensure the survival of the tribes. Women were responsible for planting many food crops, including maize, beans, and squash. Women also built and maintained homes. The homes, called long houses, were vaulted frameworks made from saplings bent into an arch. Women covered the frameworks with mats but left an opening at the top so the smoke from cooking hearths inside could escape. The homes were usually one long room, about fifty feet long, and up to twenty people lived in each home. Women also prepared food; gathered firewood; made pottery, mats, and baskets; tanned and dyed animal hides; and reared the children.

Powhatan men also had many responsiblities. They hunted, fished, and planted. And since the Powhatan traveled primarily on water, the men made canoes from trees they had hollowed out by burning the inside of the log, then scraping out the burnt wood with shells. Men were also expected to practice and prepare for war.

Powhatan Indians prayed, sang, and made offerings to several deities. Priests were held in high esteem; it was believed that they could see the future, identify criminals, and read minds.

The Indians of the Chesapeake Bay were led by a paramount chief by the name of Powhatan.

The first settlers did not bring a sufficient amount of provisions with them and had to ration food almost immediately.

For the first week or so the climate was springlike. Then the weather turned hot—very hot. The Englishmen were not accustomed to intense heat and humidity. They slaked their thirst by drinking the ale they had brought with them until it ran out; then they drank the brackish water from the streams and marshes in the area. At the same time, food supplies were running dangerously low. The expedition had boarded what were considered sufficient provisions on the ships, but the journey across the Atlantic took three months longer than anticipated, and some of the ship's crew had hoarded and wasted food.

By midsummer the settlers were rationed a half-pint of wheat and a half-pint of barley a day, a bare minimum that was infested with worms. They boiled the grain with water, then drank it. The tainted water, hot weather, and lack of food made them sick, and many became so weak that they could not work. According to an account written in June by Captain John Smith, one of the settlers, "scarce ten amongst us could either go or well stand, such extreme weakness and sickness oppressed us."[2] Newport sailed back to England for supplies; meanwhile, some desperate settlers, fed up with the conditions in Jamestown, ran away to fend for themselves. One group was found later at a place they called Point Comfort, thriving on crabs and sturgeon they had fished out of the river.

Jamestown, which was surrounded by water on three sides, became the first permanent English settlement in America.

The unfortunate location of the Jamestown settlement had created an unhealthy environment from the start. The men had selected the site in part because it was almost an island; surrounded on three sides by water, the side connected to the mainland was marshy and difficult to navigate. The settlers had determined that the isolated location would best protect them from Indian attacks. But the area was humid and mosquito-ridden, and after a rainfall the ground remained muddy for days. The tents the settlers lived in while they built houses became soggy and rotten, holding in the damp and the oppressive heat.

During the construction of the fort, natives regularly visited the settlement. They seemed so friendly that the council felt no need to ensure that the fort was attack-proof, and though many settlers were veterans of brutal wars and skilled in defense tactics, apparently none felt threatened. Perhaps because they knew the settlers were weak and their fortification inadequate, on May 27 about two hundred Indian warriors attacked the settlement. At the time, many of Jamestown's council members were away exploring the James River. A young English boy was killed in the attack, and seventeen settlers were wounded. The Indians were finally frightened away when a settler who had fled to a ship just offshore shot a limb off a tree near the fort.

As soon as the leaders returned to the settlement, they set to work strengthening the fort. By the middle of June, the triangular fort had three bulwarks, or solid supports, at each corner and four or five pieces of artillery at each bulwark. Men were stationed at each corner to watch for attacking Indians. Wingfield also made sure that each settler was armed and ready to ward off another attack.

While the settlers were bolstering the fortification, natives from some local villages came to Jamestown. They explained that they had heard of the attack and offered to help the settlers either fight the hostile natives or make peace with them. In September the same friendly natives came back to the fort with bushels of corn, which they presented to the grateful settlers. But while the natives' visits continued sporadically, the corn could not feed all of the settlers. John Smith began making expeditions to the local villages, negotiating with the natives to trade beads, copper, and iron tools for food. As the weather

After Indians attacked Jamestown, the settlers strengthened the fort and readied it for battle.

grew cold and ice formed on the river, though, Smith had to postpone his food-gathering expeditions, and the people of Jamestown were forced to endure more hardship.

## The Colony Struggles to Survive

The winter of 1607–1608 was the coldest in years. The Jamestown settlers soon found that their clothing and shelter were inadequate protection against the freezing temperatures of that Virginia winter. Each week, more of the weakened men died. The rest kept their eyes on the river, looking for the much-anticipated supply ship from England. Finally, on January 2, 1608, the ship arrived, again captained by Christopher Newport and bringing food, supplies, and 120 more settlers. The colonists unloaded the supplies and put them into the storehouse, then celebrated long into the night. But their jubilation was short-lived. On January 7 the settlement caught fire. The storehouse that contained the remaining bushels of corn, the food from the ship, and most of their supplies burned to the ground, as did several residences.

Afterward, the settlers were forced to survive on oatmeal, meal, and corn, usually mixed with water. Smith wrote that though the ship could have returned to England in fourteen days for more supplies, it instead remained fourteen weeks at Jamestown. He also complained that the crew of the ship added to the mouths that needed to be fed and greatly depleted the meager supply of food remaining. After the ship departed,

The settlers of Jamestown, unprepared for the freezing winter that lay ahead, traded with the natives for food.

To motivate the settlers to work, John Smith implemented a "no work, no food" policy.

Smith wrote that "what their discretion could spare us to make a little poor meal or two we called feasts to relish our mouths."[3]

The first colony's misfortunes were partly the result of poor planning and poor leadership. But many of the circumstances that caused so many to die were beyond anyone's control. The settlers did not know that their voyage would be delayed, or that the winter would be so cold and harsh. They did not expect a fire to destroy much of their food and other supplies. By the spring of 1608 only thirty-eight colonists remained alive. A few had been attacked by Indians while exploring the woods, but most had died of starvation or illness and infection from which their weakened bodies had little immunity.

Things began to look up, though, as the weather grew warmer and the year progressed. On the voyage from England, John Smith had offended many settlers with his brash, arrogant manner. But once the group was on land, he had slowly taken a leadership role, and in 1608 he was elected president of Jamestown. Before he became president, Smith had observed that some of the gentlemen settlers—who had been born into a class that was not accustomed to hard physical labor—had spent little time working to improve the settlement. So he implemented a "no work, no food" policy to motivate the settlers to work.

The colony slowly grew: The settlers began making pitch from pine tar, and they set up a glassworks. They planted corn in the spring and made fishing weirs and nets. By 1609 Jamestown had a church, a blockhouse, many houses, and a new storehouse. The settlers also kept Indian attacks at a minimum by a show of force: Every Saturday the men of Jamestown would gather in a clearing and march, maneuver,

# The Literature of Colonial Virginia

One reason so much is known about the founding of Virginia is that Captain John Smith and others kept detailed records of the early days of the colony. In 1608 Smith wrote *True Relation*, his history of the events of the first year or so in Virginia, which was published in England for a curious audience. Another of Smith's publications was *The Generall Historie of Virginia, New-England, and the Summer Isles, with the names of the Adventurers, Planters, and Governours from the first beginning AN. 1548 to this present 1624*, not surprisingly referred to more often as *Generall Historie*. It comprises six books and describes not only Smith's travels in Virginia but also his experiences in Bermuda and other parts of the New World. Smith added maps and illustrations to the text. He also included a section on Virginia in *The True Travels, Adventure, and Observations of Captaine John Smith, in Europe, Asia, Affrica, and America, from Anno Domini 1593 to 1629*, which was published in 1630.

In 1610 the Virginia Company of London published the pamphlets *True Declaration of the estate of the Colonie in Virginia*, based on reports written by Sir Thomas Gates. In 1616 the Virginia published another pamphlet, *Briefe Declaration of the present state of things*. Then, in 1617 John Rolfe wrote *True Relation of the State of Virginia* while he was in England with his wife, Rebecca Rolfe, formerly Pocahontas. The primary purpose of these publications was to attract investors to the company and, predictably, they have a propagandistic tone.

and shoot their muskets while a crowd of natives, most of whom had little knowledge of firepower, watched in amazement.

Although the colonists felt they were making some progress at Jamestown, the Virginia Company and King James in England were not satisfied. The colonists had explored the James River as far as they could navigate it but had made no progress in their search for a route to the Pacific Ocean. Settlers spent hours every week digging for gold, but none had been discovered. And none of the natives had been converted to Christianity. For the most part the natives and the Jamestown settlers were still wary of one another, and while the Indians found many ways to use the English tools they had traded for food, they showed no desire to adopt English customs or religion.

## The Virginia Company Steps In

The Virginia Company finally determined that the colony needed fresh leadership. The company appointed a new leader, Sir Thomas Gates, and sent him to Virginia with a new charter from King James. Gates was ordered to find out why the company's goals were not being accomplished. He was also ordered to begin Christianizing the natives using any means necessary, including kidnapping the Indian children and forcing them into English-run schools. The English were convinced that once the natives were exposed to the English way of life, they would abandon the lifestyle and traditions they had followed for hundreds—perhaps thousands—of years.

But Gates's arrival in Jamestown was delayed for almost a year because his ship, *Sea Venture*, was blown off course in a storm. While the ship, with its cargo of supplies, the new charter, and five hundred men, women, and children, made repairs in Bermuda, other English ships arrived at Jamestown, loyal to the flagship but unsure of its whereabouts.

Settlers attending a church service. Religion was an integral part of life in Jamestown.

This new group of settlers in Jamestown paid little attention to Smith. They believed their true leader was Thomas Gates and that he would arrive any day. Eventually they forced Smith to step down. He resigned but stayed in Jamestown until wounded by an accidental explosion in his powder bag. Smith, who had been president less than a year but had turned the settlement from one of despair into one of hope, was understandably reluctant to leave. But in October 1609 he went back to England, never to return to Virginia.

## The Starving Time

Now Jamestown had no real leader. Smith was gone and Gates was absent, so council member George Percy took over. Under his orders, some settlers stepped up their search for gold, neglecting the constant need to plant and tend crops, fish, or hunt for food for the colony. Many of the newly arrived English gentlemen contributed little if any work to the colony; unused to physical labor, they were inept at construction, mining, and farming, and Percy was not able to motivate them to work. In contrast to Smith, who had enforced strict, sometimes extremely harsh, but effective policies, Percy seemed to have little control over the settlers. The colony began to languish,

John Smith, who became president of Jamestown in 1608, was forced to resign a year later.

and although the nearby rivers and the Chesapeake Bay teemed with sea life, the settlers began to starve. They became so desperate that they ate shoe leather, clothing, all of the animals (including their pets), mice, snakes, and roots. Some of the colonists even ate the bodies of those who had died. The settlers later referred to this as "the starving time."

John Smith might have attempted again to trade with the Indians for food, but Percy did not know quite what to do. Smith had earned the respect

As hopes of becoming rich in a new land faded, many settlers sat idle and played games in the street to pass the time.

of the natives, but the great chief did not have the same respect for Percy. William Symonds, one of the settlers, later wrote about this time, "Now we all found the loss of Captain Smith; yea, his greatest maligners could now curse his loss. As for corn provision and contribution from the savages, we had nothing but mortal wounds, with clubs and arrows." Desperation drove the settlers to horrific measures: One man killed his wife and ate most of her body before his crime was discovered and he was executed. Symonds placed the blame for these tragedies squarely on the settlers, saying, "It were too vile to say, and scarce to be believed what we endured. But the occasion was our own, for want of providence, industry, and government and not the barrenness and defect of the country, as is generally supposed."[4]

More than five hundred colonists lived in Jamestown when John Smith left in October 1609. By early spring of 1610, only sixty settlers remained. Some had fled to Indian villages, where they knew they could at least get food. Other small groups of settlers ran off to fend for themselves and were never heard from again. But most of the settlers died from sickness and starvation. Dreams of finding gold and becoming rich were forgotten, and most of the settlers spent their days in idleness, bowling in the streets to pass the time.

Just as early settlers decided to abandon Jamestown, provisions and more settlers arrived from England.

On May 24, 1610, Gates and his passengers finally arrived in Jamestown. In less than two weeks, he decided that the situation was hopeless and that the remaining settlers should abandon Jamestown and return to England. On June 7 the settlers boarded ships and began to sail down the river. But as they were leaving, they were intercepted by English ships carrying Thomas West, Baron de la Warr; three hundred more settlers; and a year's supply of food. De la Warr had been appointed by the Virginia Company to take over leadership of Jamestown. Under his leadership, the level of sickness and starvation that had occurred in years past would finally be overcome. The colony was saved.

## Chapter Two

# The Colony Grows

As Jamestown was rebuilding, the Virginia Company continued to struggle to make a profit. Its members resigned themselves to the fact that neither gold nor silver would be found anywhere near Jamestown, and they turned to the exploitation of other commodities.

Europeans at the time were indulging in a new habit: tobacco smoking. The Spanish had discovered tobacco in the West Indies and brought it to Europe. Spain, long a rival of England, sold this tobacco to London merchants at high prices. The rising popularity of tobacco gave Jamestown settler John Rolfe an idea. He imported tobacco seeds from the Caribbean and planted them in Virginia. This proved to be one of the most significant acts in the settlement's short history, for it was to be tobacco that made Virginia into a profitable colony. While Virginians grew tobacco, tobacco grew Virginia.

### The Seeds of a Colony

Rolfe harvested his first crop of tobacco in 1612 and asked his neighbors to try it. They said that Rolfe's tobacco "smoked pleasant, sweete and strong."[5] Next, Rolfe sent some to England. There it was deemed acceptable, and the English encouraged the production of more tobacco.

The people of Jamestown quickly became tobacco crazed. They planted tobacco everywhere. As settlers became more comfortable living among the Indians, they began to move away from the fort and

Because tobacco grew so well in Virginia, plantations cropped up all over the new colony.

build houses along the James River, clearing land and planting tobacco. Thus the Virginia plantation system was born.

In 1614 Virginia entered the world tobacco market. Rolfe continued to experiment and improve his crop, and soon grew tobacco that rivaled that of Spain. In 1615 he shipped twenty thousand pounds of tobacco to England. By 1619 Virginia had begun to use tobacco as currency; it would continue to do so for the next two hundred years.

## The Headright System

The profitability of tobacco caused a rekindling of interest in Virginia. For several years people in England had been reluctant to move to the colony. They had heard of the disease, the hostile Indians, and the starvation that they might encounter. To encourage more settlers, in 1618 the Virginia Company instituted a headright program: Those who settled in Virginia would receive fifty acres of land if they paid their own passage and fifty more acres for each additional person's passage they paid.

People who could not afford to pay their own passage became the indentured servants of their benefactors, working off their passage in terms that usually lasted from four to seven years. Besides passage, they were entitled to food, clothing, and shelter once they landed in

# The 1622 Massacre

The marriage of John Rolfe to Pocahontas, daughter of the great Indian leader Powhatan, resulted in a time of relative peace between the Powhatan Indians (known to the English by the same name as their leader) and the English settlers. When Powhatan died in 1618, tribal rule passed to Opechancanough, his younger brother. The colony's new governor, Francis Wyatt, ratified a peace treaty with Opechancanough in late 1621. Confident of their safety, the settlers no longer carried arms with them wherever they went and invited Powhatan people to stay in their homes.

But that all changed on March 16, 1622. As they often did, many Indians came early to the plantations to barter furs and corn for imported English goods. But on this morning, the natives suddenly and violently turned on the English. By the end of the day, 349 settlers were dead, and twenty-five plantations around Jamestown were burned.

News of the massacre did not reach England until June. England responded angrily; the Virginia Company called for revenge. In *American Genesis* by Alden Vaughan, Edward Waterhouse of the Virginia Company is quoted as writing that the massacre resulted in the English feeling that, they "May now by right of warre, and law of Nations, invade the Country, and destroy them who sought to destroy us." At the end of 1622 and into 1623, bands of Englishmen sought out the Powhatan, killing them and their animals and destroying their crops. They were successful at driving out the natives: By 1669 the populations of Powhatan people in Virginia had dropped from an estimated fourteen thousand in 1607 to only eighteen hundred, and by 1772 many tribes in the Powhatan confederacy were reported to be extinct.

The Powhatan attacked Jamestown, killing 349 men, women, and children.

Virginia. When the term of their indenture ended, they gained their independence and continued to work for wages until they earned enough money to buy land and plant tobacco. This method of emigration became the standard; historians estimate that by the middle of the seventeenth century, 75 percent of all landowners had come to Virginia as indentured servants. This group of colonists eventually developed into Virginia's middle class, often called the yeoman class. Yeoman farmers were generally considered to be planters who owned from fifty to five hundred acres.

Former indentured servants who could not afford land either continued to work as hired hands or became tenant farmers, raising subsistence crops on small plots of land they rented from wealthier planters. Some went west to the frontier and became Virginia's poor, squatting on land until they were forced off.

After gaining their independence, indentured servants could earn money to buy land and grow tobacco.

Because the soil was fertile around the Tidewater area, planters built plantations along the rivers.

With this system as a base, the colony continued to grow in and around the Tidewater area. This coastal plain region around the James, York, Rappahannock, and Potomac Rivers was ideal for growing tobacco. The soil around its rivers was fertile, and with numerous waterways nearby, planters could easily transport the heavy hogsheads into which tobacco was packed. Planters built plantations along the rivers, and ships from England sailed across the Atlantic and up the river to the plantation's wharf. There, the hogsheads were loaded onto the ships for the return trip to England.

## The Development of Towns

Because planters sold their tobacco at their own private wharves or at wharves built by British merchants, few commercial centers were established in colonial Tidewater Virginia. A few small villages were established, including Hampton, located where the Chesapeake Bay and the James River meet, and West Point, at the mouth of the York River, but each of these communities housed only about one hundred

As the center of slave trade for the colony, Yorktown became one of the most prominent towns in seventeenth-century Virginia.

residents. The most prominent towns settled in the 1600s were Williamsburg, which became the colony's capital in 1699, Yorktown, and Norfolk. Yorktown was the center of Chesapeake slave trade, while Norfolk received goods such as beef, flour, and lumber from farmers in southern Virginia and North Carolina and shipped them to England.

Few shops and artisans thrived in colonial Virginia because the British government discouraged the development of colonial manufacturing. Instead, British merchants encouraged planters to order goods directly from England through them. The merchants calculated an amount of credit allotted each planter based on the market value of the planter's tobacco. Planters ordered what they needed, and when the tobacco-laden ships arrived in England, the merchants or their agents filled the order and shipped it to the planters on the next Virginia-bound vessel.

## The Rise of the Planter-Merchant

As the tobacco industry grew, more and more land was used up, because a field could be planted with tobacco for only about seven years before the soil was depleted. Planters were forced to let depleted fields lie fallow for up to twenty years, and successive crops were not

# Bacon's Rebellion

In western Virginia in 1675 and 1676, Indian attacks against settlers were becoming so frequent and severe that the settlers begged Governor Berkeley for assistance. He promised to help them, but as they waited, hundreds more were killed. Frustrated by the delay, Nathaniel Bacon Jr., a relative of Berkeley's and a member of Virginia's council (a group of men appointed by Parliament to help govern Virginia), asked the governor for a commission to fight the Indians. Berkeley refused. Bacon then gathered a band of frontiersmen and attacked the Occaneechee, killing more than a hundred.

Berkeley charged Bacon with treason, removed him from the council, and had him arrested. Bacon admitted his guilt, so he was granted a pardon and promised a commission. Time passed and he did not receive his commission, so Bacon and his men marched to Jamestown and surrounded the statehouse. Berkeley stormed out of the statehouse and shouted taunts at Bacon, who calmly told his men to aim their guns at statehouse windows. Berkeley backed down and gave Bacon his commission. Bacon and his men left, and Berkeley almost immediately had all of them declared traitors and rebels. Bacon and his followers—whose number was growing to include many assembly members—demanded that the governor surrender the government, because his behavior was treasonous. All they were doing, they protested, was trying to save the loyal subjects of the king who were being murdered by Indians. Berkeley sent forces to confront Bacon's, but when faced with Bacon's army, Berkeley's men fled.

Suddenly, Bacon became sick and died a few days later. Without their leader, his followers disbanded. But many of those who survived were punished: About twenty-three of his supporters were hanged for treason. Many historians believe Bacon's Rebellion was a significant event in Virginia's history, a message to royal governors that that control was limited.

as productive as the first one. Unaware of modern farming methods of fertilization or crop rotation, planters simply bought more land and cleared it to grow tobacco. At first they took all the land along the riverbanks. Then they were forced to move inland. But planters who did not live adjacent to a river faced a transportation problem: How would they get the hogsheads of tobacco to the wharves where English ships would take it to market?

Riverside planters had the answer: They began to act as merchants for the inland planters, allowing the planters to ship tobacco from their wharves for a fee. The planter-merchants became intermediaries, or middlemen, for the inland planters. Many also opened small stores and began to sell goods they had ordered from England. Because there were so few general stores during the colony's early years, the inland planters were forced to purchase products from planter-merchants, who in turn made a good profit. Many of these planter-merchants made their fortunes this way. They rose to become the wealthy planters who formed the gentry class of the late seventeenth and eighteenth centuries.

Because delivering tobacco from inland plantations was difficult, growers paid a fee to use the wharves of riverside planters.

## The Labor Shortage

Once the good Tidewater land was either purchased or depleted, planters began to move farther to the north and west to the fall line at Richmond. (The fall line is the boundary between the Atlantic coastal plain—the Tidewater—and the higher plains of the Piedmont farther west.) Former indentured servants bought up the cheaper land along rivers in the Piedmont region, as did wealthy planters looking for new tobacco fields.

A labor shortage occurred when Britain began enforcing the Navigation Act in 1660. Originally enacted in 1624 after the Virginia Company dissolved and Virginia became a royal colony, the act declared that all Virginia tobacco must be shipped only on English-owned ships and sold through London. It was not strictly enforced, though, until 1660, when King Charles II added heavy taxes and duties on tobacco to the act to increase England's revenues.

Planters, particularly small-scale yeomen, struggled to pay the extra fees imposed by the Navigation Act. Wealthy planters reacted to the extra fees by buying up more land. More land meant they could grow more tobacco and make more money to cover the extra expenses imposed by the Navigation Act. More land also meant that they would need more laborers. But workers were becoming harder to find. Many of the indentured servants who had come to Virginia earlier had already gained their freedom, and fewer new workers were coming to Virginia; the economy in England was steadily improving, and many prospective laborers instead found work in their homeland. Finally, the planters, with newly cleared fields ready to be planted with tobacco, turned to slaves.

## Slavery in Virginia

The first slaves came to Virginia in 1619, Africans held on a Dutch ship that was blown off course. They were left in Jamestown, where it is believed they were treated as indentured servants. A few African slaves were brought to Virginia in succeeding decades, but most planters did not like the idea of slavery. However, when Virginia's legislature, called the House of Burgesses, legalized slavery in 1661, planters began widespread adoption of the practice.

Wealthy plantation owners bought slaves to work in the tobacco fields.

By 1671, there were 2,000 African slaves in Virginia. Three thousand more were brought to the Chesapeake area in the 1690s. In the eighteenth century, more slaves were imported; by 1715, there were approximately 23,000 slaves in Virginia, compared with about 72,500 whites. The ability of wealthy planters to acquire slaves dealt a severe blow to those lesser planters who could not afford slaves; the more slaves planters had, the more tobacco they could produce and the more money they could make to buy up more land and more slaves. Small-scale planters, on the other hand, could afford neither land nor slaves, so their farms remained small, as did their pocketbooks.

Another blow to the small-scale planter came in 1730, when the House of Burgesses passed the Virginia Tobacco Act to regulate the industry and raise tobacco prices. The goal of the act was to eliminate "bad and trash tobacco" from export. It stated that every hogshead marked for export would first have to be inspected to make sure the quality of the tobacco was high. The act had a detrimental effect on small planters, who often stuffed poor-quality "trash" tobacco into the center of their hogsheads to add to the weight. Because poorer planters could not afford to buy the land and slaves that wealthier planters could purchase, they felt they had no choice but to stuff the hogheads with trash to make it look as if they had produced more tobacco than they had. They were trying to compete with the wealthier planters, whose tobacco was of higher quality because they had the fresh land and workers to maintain the crops adequately.

The yeoman farmers worked hard to compete with wealthy landowners, but by the middle of the eighteenth century the income of the small-scale yeoman planters had greatly diminished. Colonial historian Thomas J. Wertenbaker says that the ability of the wealthy in Virginia to control the land "transformed Virginia and the South from a land of hard-working, self-respecting yeoman to a land of slaves and slaveholders."[6]

## The Changing Agricultural Climate

But the act seemed to have its desired results. After about 1740, tobacco prices rose. As a result, British merchants were able to extend even more credit to the gentry, who in turn spent more money on British products.

Towns also grew during this time. Alexandria, Fredericksburg, Richmond, and Petersburg became commercial centers for the

As Virginia was transformed into a land of slaves and slaveholders, small-scale yeoman planters could not compete.

regions beyond Tidewater. By 1769 about 600 people lived in Richmond, a tobacco marketing and inspection center, and its population tripled by 1782. Alexandria was also a bustling tobacco marketing center: By 1790, it boasted a population of 2,750.

Virginia's Piedmont region grew as well, as thousands moved to the area. Tobacco merchants there supplied credit, and many plantations were established. Into the second half of the eighteenth century, Piedmont grew to be much like Tidewater, as wealthy planters bought land and planted tobacco, forcing poor planters farther west and south.

But by the mid-1700s, the economic system that had ruled in Tidewater Virginia for more than a hundred years was weakening. Yeoman planters were forced to turn to other crops to survive. The British economy was suffering as Britain waged an expensive war with France (the Seven Years' War, 1754–1763; in North America called the French and Indian War), and gentry planters who had for years gone deep into debt to British merchants offering credits were being asked to pay up. Planters who had lent money to other planters began calling for payment of debts, a crisis for some planters who had borrowed way beyond their means and could not pay back their creditors. In 1764 Virginian John Baylor bemoaned his colony's situation, writing, "Poor Virginia, what art thou reduced to, held in scorn & derision by the merchants of great Britain & torn to pieces by theirs & our country law suits."[7] Some planters scrambling to pay their debts sold lottery tickets to their neighbors, with the prize being the plantation. Benjamin Johnson advertised such a lottery in 1768:

> The reason of my selling on this method is (I assure the public) to pay my debts, and prevent imposition; and [to avoid] that too prevailing custom falling on me, which had on many in this colony, i.e. selling estates by execution at half value. I hope it will meet with applause and encouragement.[8]

## The Fall of the Tobacco Economy

Most gentry planters managed to survive the crisis. But all planters, regardless of their debt to British merchants, were growing tired of roller-coaster tobacco prices, made even more unstable by bad weather

Even though the market was unstable, ships continued to deliver tobacco to England.

and pest damage to the crops. In 1770, after his tobacco crop was attacked by grasshoppers, Landon Carter wrote, "We must submit to all such destruction and do as well as we can, but I believe it will be difficult under such a staple to make a tollerable substinence."[9] Shortly afterward, Carter wrote, "I cannot help observing as I have before done that this climate is so changing [that] unless it return to its former state Virginia will be no Tobacco Colony soon."[10]

Many planters apparently agreed. By the 1770s wheat was the second most widely grown crop in Virginia. While most planters had been growing at least some wheat for generations, they were only now becoming aware that it might be more marketable than tobacco. Accordingly, in 1774 William Allason wrote that he was glad to hear the grain harvest was good that year, because "most planters had gone more on it [wheat] than heretofore, their dependence on Tobacco being much lessened."[11]

Tobacco may no longer have been king in Virginia, but tobacco is what allowed Virginia to grow from a population of 700 in 1618 to 284,000 in 1754 and, by 1790, to more than 700,000 people. Revenue from tobacco built homes, courthouses, churches, and villages; tobacco was woven into the very fiber of colonial Virginia, and it shaped not only the economy of Virginia, but many other aspects of the colony as well.

## Chapter Three

# Daily Life in Colonial Virginia

The cultivation and marketing of tobacco guided almost every aspect of life for most residents of colonial Virginia. But while nearly all slaves, poor farmers, yeoman farmers, and wealthy planters were involved in the cultivation of tobacco, their activities and roles in Virginia society were markedly different.

### The Life of a Slave

Slaves lived lives of great hardship and deprivation. They worked in the fields from dawn to dusk, six days a week, women alongside men. Slave children began working part-time between the ages of seven and nine, and their daily labor increasingly lengthened as they aged. Considered property, slaves were subject to rape and beatings, and could be bought and sold at a master's discretion, sometimes separated from family members forever.

The homes of slaves were usually one-room wooden shacks called "quarters," usually located as far from the main house as plantation size allowed. Each residence was about sixteen by sixteen feet and typically had a mud-daubed fireplace and floors of packed dirt. The quarters were not comfortable: Slaves usually slept on straw bedding and sat on rough benches or furniture made from barrels.

In the common yard outside the quarters slaves gathered and ground grain on a grindstone or in a hand mill to make flour. They often raised livestock, which lived in the common yard or in a small pasture nearby. Slaves could usually cultivate crops of their own in the evenings and on Sunday, their one day off, in small fields close to their quarters.

## The Life of a Poor Farmer

The lives of poor farmers were also difficult. Poor farmers in colonial Virginia—those who owned no land—often squatted on land in the frontier. For most of the colony's history, the frontier began at the fall line—the point where rivers are no longer navigable—where Richmond is today. Poor farmers and their families worked hard to survive. They built small wooden homes and owned perhaps one cow, a goat, a horse, and some chickens and ducks. Poor farmers often grew little or no tobacco. The distance from their farms to any port precluded their being able to transport hogsheads of tobacco.

Slaves lived with great hardship, working six days a week from dawn to dusk and living in one-room shacks called "quarters."

But even as outsiders poor farmers were still affected by the tobacco industry. While they grew crops to fill the needs of their households, with a little bit left over to sell if they could find a buyer (which was difficult, since neighbors were few and far between), they could not afford to enter the tobacco market as growers or landowners. They were at the mercy of the wealthy tobacco planters who eventually bought up the land they lived on, forcing them to seek out new places to squat farther west or south.

## The Life of a Yeoman Planter

The lifestyle of yeoman planters was molded by their determination to make a profit by growing tobacco. In the seventeenth century, nearly every planter in Virginia could have been considered a yeoman planter. But by the eighteenth century, a small group of planters had risen to the level of gentry, and the yeoman planter was decidedly middle class. Of his boyhood in New Kent County on a yeoman farm, Devereux Jarratt wrote:

> None of my ancestors, on either side, were rich or great, but had the character of honesty and industry, by which they lived in credit among their neighbors, free from real want, and above the frowns of the world. . . . They always had plenty of plain food and raiment [clothing], wholesome and good, suitable to their humble station, and the times in which they lived. Our food was altogether the produce of the farm, or plantation. [12]

In both centuries, yeoman planters lived modestly in wood-frame houses of one or two stories. One-story homes usually had a loft where children slept and goods were stored. Furnishings were simple. A large table dominated the main living space, and family members sat on rough wooden chairs or benches. In the seventeenth and early eighteenth centuries families owned little other furniture besides bedsteads; they might have a blanket chest or chest of drawers. They owned a few pieces of linen, such as sheets and a tablecloth, and ate from earthenware dishes.

By the middle of the eighteenth century many middle-class yeoman planters could afford a more comfortable lifestyle.

By the middle of the eighteenth century, many middle-class Virginians could afford more elegant furnishings. They purchased porcelain plates and teapots, linens, even mirrors. Furniture became easier to obtain, and they might have a small occasional table on which to place a candlestick or to serve tea. They began to add cushions to their hard chairs and benches.

Still, many everyday amenities were lacking. Candles were expensive to make, so many common planters went to bed when it was dark and rose when the sun came up. Because water had to be carried from a well, spring, or town pump, most colonial Virginians bathed infrequently, and bathroom facilities were contained in a small outbuilding usually located behind the house.

## The Life of the Gentry

Colonial Virginia's wealthiest group of planters, the gentry, composed about 10 percent of the population. Many were descended from yeoman planters who had managed to acquire a great deal of land in the seventeenth century; others were members of favored families who had been granted large plots of land by one of the royal governors of Virginia. Land ownership meant power; as Virginia's aristocracy, they controlled the colony's government and economy.

Gentleman planters had a huge amount of responsibility but did not toil in the fields. Instead, most of their time was engaged in writing letters, conducting government business, and managing the plantation. A plantation was like a small village, with outbuildings for cooking, smoking meat, making hogsheads, blacksmithing, and other functions. Wealthy planters took great pride in the communities they developed, and they accepted the responsibility for everything that happened in those communities. Many expressed the notion of *noblesse oblige*, the idea that privilege and high rank carried a responsibility to be generous and honorable toward others, especially the less privileged.

Although gentlemen were responsible for the management of large plantations and the demands of public life, in general they led enviable lives. In the 1720s William Byrd wrote of the rather idyllic life of a Virginia gentleman:

Even though they were responsible for the management of large plantations, the gentry lived enviable lives.

# The Byrd Family

The Byrd family was among the more prominent in colonial Virginia. The first member of the family came to Virginia from England in about 1670 as an Indian trader, exchanging rum, ammunition, guns, hatchets, and cloth for furs, deer and beaverskins, rare herbs, and minerals. Byrd was also a tobacco planter and dealt in indentured servants and African slaves. Eventually he became a member of the House of Burgesses and the Council of State.

William Byrd II was an educated plantation owner.

His son, William Byrd II (1674–1744), was a literate man who acquired more than thirty-six hundred books in his personal library. Byrd went to England to be educated when he was seven, then studied law at London's Middle Temple. Upon his father's death, Byrd inherited twenty-six thousand acres and two hundred slaves. He returned to Virginia, where he was a member of the House of Burgesses and, later, the Council of State. He supervised the construction of the mansion at Westover, one of the great plantations of the eighteenth century, and he founded Richmond in 1737.

William Byrd III did not follow in the footsteps of his father and grandfather. He inherited almost 180,000 acres, but was a voracious gambler and drinker. He was forced to sell hundreds of slaves to pay his gambling debts, and in 1777 he shot and killed himself.

But the Byrd family endured. One of its most famous desendants was Richard E. Byrd, best known for his explorations to the South Pole. Harry Flood Byrd served as governor of Virginia from 1926 to 1930 and U.S. senator from 1933 to 1965, and his son, Harry Jr., was a U.S. senator from 1965 to 1983.

Like one of the patriarchs I have my flocks and my herds, my bond-men and bond-women, and every sort of trade amongst my own servants, so that I live in a kind of independence on everyone but providence. . . . My doors are open to everybody . . . and a half-crown will rest undisturbed in my pocket for many moons together. . . . We sit securely under our vines and fig-trees . . . [and] can rest securely in our beds with all doors and windows open, and yet find everything exactly in place the next morning. We can travel all over the country by night and by day, unguarded and unarmed.[13]

As the eighteenth century progressed, wealthy planters acquired more slaves and therefore more leisure time, and many spent it engaged in activities that were frowned on by visitors or newcomers to Virginia. One immigrant, James Reid, exclaimed in 1769 that the typical gentleman of the Chesapeake region "drinks, fights, bullies, curses, swears, whores, games, sings, whistles, dances, jumps, capers, runs, talks baudy, visits Gentlemen he never saw, had the rendez-vous with the Ladies he never spoke to . . . eats voraciously, sleeps, snores, and takes snuff."[14] Another visitor, Philadelphian Ebenezer Hazard, was surprised to see in 1775 that Virginians were "much addicted to Gaming, drinking, swearing, horse-racing [and] cockfighting."[15] Indeed, after a long day sitting at a desk going over accounts or corresponding with London merchants, the gentlemen of colonial Virginia often went to the local tavern to gamble, drink, eat, and socialize with other gentlemen.

## Plantation Homes

As planters grew wealthier, their homes became larger and more impressive. Many planters' homes of the early eighteenth century were designed in the popular Georgian style, constructed of bricks made in the plantation's own kiln. The homes were two or three stories and had a large central hallway. On the first floor were formal rooms for entertaining guests and for everyday living. Bedrooms were on the second floor. Bathroom facilities usually consisted of a chamberpot and a pitcher and washbasin arranged in the bedroom for removal by servants, who carried water from a pump or well into the main house.

Because of the heat a kitchen produced and the risk of fire, cooking was done in an outbuilding. Often the kitchen was connected to the main house by a tunnel; such was the case at Berkeley Plantation and at Monticello, Thomas Jefferson's home.

The gentry bought their furnishings from England. Homes were furnished with sofas and chairs upholstered in silk brocade or fine tapestry. Nearly every room had a fireplace, often with a carved wood mantel and framework. The floors were made from wide wood planks and covered with imported rugs. The dining table was laid with white linen and sparkling crystal imported from England or other European countries. Food was served in delicate china and accompanied by French wines. The family and guests of gentlemen were served coffee and tea regularly.

Many grand plantation homes were on the banks of a river and had sweeping lawns and terraced gardens. Others were built on hilltops. One visitor to a plantation in Albemarle County described the landscape this way:

As the gentry grew wealthier, their homes became larger and more lavish.

The house that we reside in is situated upon an eminence, commanding a prospect of nearly thirty miles around it, and the face of the country appears as an immense forest, interspersed with various plantations, four or five miles distant from each other; on these there is a dwelling-house in the center, with kitchens, smoke-house, and out-houses detached, and from the various buildings, each plantation has the appearance of a small village; at some little distance from the houses, are peach and apple orchards, &c. and scattered over the plantations are the negroes huts and tobacco-houses, which are largely built of wood. [16]

## Government in Colonial Virginia

The power of wealthy planters extended beyond their own plantations. The gentry were involved in every aspect of colonial government, acting as assemblymen, justices of the peace, sheriffs, and vestrymen. These offices were closely held for generations, often passed down from father to son. Members of the House of Burgesses were elected officials, but all other office holders were appointed.

The old capital at Williamsburg where the House of Burgesses met.

Members of the House of Burgesses were elected officials.

After 1670 only white men who owned land could vote in colonial Virginia, so gentlemen and yeomen exclusively voted in elections. The two groups had a reciprocal relationship. Yeomen deferred to and cast votes for the gentry, and in return the gentry were expected to protect the rights of the common planter. If yeoman planters knew a gentleman would not defend their rights, they made it clear that they would not support that gentleman in an election.

The House of Burgesses, the governor's council, and the governor made up the General Assembly. According to Charles M. Andrews, it was decided in 1639 that "a royal colony should be, in part at least, a self-administering community, with a governor and council appointed in England and a representative assembly chosen by the freemen or freeholders in the colony." [17] The legislators of colonial Virginia made and passed laws and acts that would affect the lives of those who lived in the colony, often favoring laws that protected the interests of the aristocracy.

The General Assembly met to pass laws that affected the lives of those who lived in the colony.

The aristocracy also held the offices of county commissioners, or justices of the peace, as they were later called. They were responsible for administering county government, trying cases, and punishing criminals who committed misdemeanors. The commissioner was appointed by the governor and his council, as was the vestryman. The role of the vestry was to allocate parish taxes, disburse poor relief, and oversee morality. However, as a result of the loose structure of the Anglican Church in Virginia, vestrymen rarely enforced morality codes.

## The Role of the Church in Colonial Virginia

Indeed, while the Anglican Church was the official state church of Virginia, its influence did not extend to the whole of society. Because of the great distance between plantations, parishes were huge. And there were few clergy, particularly in the seventeenth century; some had to travel from parish to parish, taking weeks to cover all their territory. The Anglican Church expected adults to attend church services at least once a month. But some families had to travel nearly one hundred miles to reach the closest church.

As a result, church attendance was sparse when the weather was bad. But in fair weather, many families did attend church. The weekly church service was both a religious and a social event. After the service, people stood around and talked, discussing business and inviting one another to dinner. While their parents talked, children played together, and adolescents gossiped and flirted.

## Education in Colonial Virginia

Because they lived so far apart, children in colonial Virginia saw their neighbors only at church services and other ceremonies or during celebrations such as balls and wedding receptions. They were often too isolated to attend school; in 1661 the Reverend Roger Green wrote in a pamphlet about Virginia, "Their almost general want of schools for the education of their children is another consequent of their scattered planting."[18]

Parishioners attend a service at an Anglican church, a religious and social event.

Some planters ensured that their children were educated by hiring tutors to live on the plantation and teach their children. Girls were taught how to read, but not always how to write. Most of their lessons concerned domestic duties and social graces, such as sewing and deportment.

# The College of William and Mary

In July 1690 the clergy of Virginia met and Reverend James Blair, Commissary, presented several propositions that provided for advanced education in the colony. In 1691 the General Assembly petitioned England for a charter for the college. William and Mary, who reigned together over England as king and queen, approved a charter for the school in 1693. The goals of the school were to educate men who wished to be Anglican clergy or civil servants. The College of William and Mary is second only to Harvard University as the oldest college in America and is the only American college chartered by the Crown.

James Blair was made president of the college for life, and a board of trustees, selected by the governor, was appointed. Middle Plantation, now called Williamsburg, was chosen as the site for the college. Famed architect Sir Christopher Wren designed the building, and the foundations were laid in 1695. By 1700 the college president, two masters (professors), and several students were living on campus. Some early graduates of the school were future presidents Thomas Jefferson, James Monroe, and John Tyler, as well as John Marshall, future Supreme Court chief justice. The college burned down in 1705, but was promptly rebuilt.

Wren Building at the College of William and Mary.

William and Mary was supported by the Crown until 1776. After that, it was supported by private funds until 1906, when it became state-supported. The college became coed in 1918 and became a university in 1967, but retained its original name.

The education of boys was taken more seriously. Boys of the gentry were expected to study Latin, Greek, and mathematics along with reading and writing. Boys also learned the family business from their fathers, accompanying them on visits to other plantations and to court sessions. Some sons of wealthier planters were sent to England to be formally educated. The British merchant who worked with the family usually arranged for the boy's education and living arrangements.

Children of both gentry and yeoman sometimes attended "Old Field Schools." Groups of planters got together, built the schools on fallow fields, and hired a teacher. Sometimes group lessons were conducted in a planter's home. The children of the planters all attended the school, although it was more common for the children of yeoman planters to be educated by their parents at home and taught reading and writing.

The poorest white children were taught reading and writing if their parents could read and write. Poor children were also educated as part of their indenture or apprenticeship, usually in the homes of the people to whom they were indentured. Occasionally, they had the opportunity to attend what were called "free schools." The first of these was established by the will of Benjamin Syms, who gave two acres of land for a school in Elizabeth City County. In that same county in 1659 Thomas Eaton left land and proceeds from cattle to be used for a school adjoining that of Syms. In 1805 these two schools were combined into one, called Hampton Academy.

Other similar endowments were made throughout Virginia. Robert Beverley wrote in 1705, "There are large tracts of land, house and other things granted to free schools for the education of children in many parts of the country . . . schools founded by legacies of well-inclined gentlemen, and management . . . left to direction of county court or the vestry of respective parishes." [19]

This way of life in Virginia was maintained for at least a century amid mounting political unrest in all the British colonies. Americans were tired of British taxation and other interference in their increasingly independent affairs. Change was on its way.

## Chapter Four

# Virginia's Role in the American Revolution

For the colony's first 150 years, Virginians lived off the land. Poor farmers spent days toiling in the sun and the rain, growing vegetables and fruit and tending livestock. Yeoman farmers joined their one or two slaves in the fields, planting, harvesting, and processing tobacco while their wives and children tended to vegetable crops and livestock. Gentleman farmers not only governed the colony but also oversaw activity on plantations that sometimes comprised thousands of acres.

Virginia had grown and prospered, and its people had become self-sufficient and, for all intents and purposes, self-governing. They valued their independence and their way of life, but they did not realize just how valuable this way of life was to them until it was threatened. The threat came from the country to which many of them formally pledged allegiance: England.

When forced to commit themselves to Virginia or England, however, most Virginians confidently chose Virginia and independence. For most, the choice was easy. They were farmers, tied to the land they had come to love. They were managers, overseeing a staff of one or a staff of one thousand. They were leaders whose ancestors had seen Virginia grow from a tiny, struggling settlement to a thriving colony. Virginians, on the whole, were unshaken in their belief that they could govern themselves—and that they had the right to do so.

## The Stamp Act

While Great Britain had been controlling the colonies in various ways for years, in 1765 it went too far, imposing the Stamp Act, which required Americans to buy stamps to affix to deeds, mortgages, liquor licenses, law licenses, playing cards, and almanacs, newspapers, and other publications. The money from the stamps would help pay for the British troops stationed in the colonies.

All the colonies protested the Stamp Act, but Virginia did so with the most force. Patrick Henry, a newly elected member of the House of Burgesses, was determined that colonial legislators should pass resolves against the Stamp Act and any other taxation imposed upon Virginia by Great Britain. He had written the resolves himself, and he

Patrick Henry addresses the Virginia Assembly.

introduced them to a less than half-full House on May 30. The first four resolves said, basically, that as British citizens—for the people of the colonies were technically under British rule and, therefore, subject to the laws of Great Britain—the people of Virginia could not be taxed without representation in Parliament, Britain's legislature.

The four resolves passed easily. But Henry was not finished; he had a bold fifth resolution to announce. The resolution is not mentioned in the records of the House, but it was later published in several newspapers in the following form:

> Resolved, Therefore that the General assembly of this Colony have the only and sole exclusive Right and Power to lay Taxes and Impositions upon the Inhabitants of this Colony and that every Attempt to vest such Power in any Person or Persons whatsoever other than the General Assembly aforesaid has a manifest Tendency to destroy British as well as American Freedom.[20]

This resolution divided the House, because it stated that only the General Assembly of Virginia (which consisted of the House of Burgesses, the governor's council, and the governor), not British Parliament, had the right to tax the people of Virginia. This statement, many felt, went too far. After all, Virginia was still a British colony.

Because it does not appear in the official record, the resolution was most certainly not passed. But for some reason, the resolution was published in newspapers as if it had passed. One newspaper, the *Newport* (Rhode Island) *Mercury*, even published a sixth resolution, one that stated nearly the same thing—that the citizens of Virginia were to obey no law that imposed taxes except laws made by the General Assembly:

> Resolved, That his Majesty's liege People, the Inhabitants of this Colony, are not bound to yield Obedience to any Law or Ordinance whatever, designed to impose any Taxation whatsoever upon them, other than the Laws or Ordinances of the General Assembly aforesaid.[21]

Colonial newspapers published Patrick Henry's five resolutions.

Another resolution was also printed in some newspapers. Its strong language, implying that Parliament was now an enemy of the colony of Virginia, probably shocked some colonists:

> That any Person who shall, by Speaking, or Writing, assert or maintain, That any Person or Persons, other than the General Assembly of this Colony, with such Consent as aforesaid, have any Right or Authority to lay or impose any Tax whatever on the Inhabitants thereof, shall be deemed, AN ENEMY TO HIS MAJESTY'S COLONY.[22]

This resolution is also not mentioned in the House record and was almost certainly not passed. But many in other colonies who read the printed version believed that because it was published, it had passed, and a spark of rebellion was ignited. In reaction to Virginia's resolves, eight other colonies also introduced resolves against the Stamp Act.

An angry mob protests the Stamp Act.

To many, the Stamp Act was a warning that Great Britain was prepared to take away more freedoms from the colonists. Landon Carter, a Virginia plantation owner, wrote to the newspaper *Virginia Gazette* that the Stamp Act "was the first resolution to enslave us." [23] Because the act was so unpopular, Parliament was forced to repeal it in 1766. Afterward, most colonies sent letters to England's king, thanking him for repealing the act. But Virginia sent no such letter; historian Robert Middlekauff writes that "in refusing to send thanks to the king, the [House of] Burgesses maintained the integrity it had shown a year earlier" [24] [when the assembly passed the resolutions in 1765 condemning the act.] While other colonies expressed their gratitude to the king for repealing the Stamp Act, the people of Virginia believed that such an expression would weaken their stance against taxation without representation. After all, Parliament could not expect them to obey any law they had no part in making. Relaying thanks to the king would send the message that Parliament had the right to impose such laws in the first place.

## The Townshend and Quartering Acts

The House of Burgesses continued to maintain its integrity when Britain issued its next order of taxation. In 1767 Parliament imposed the Townshend Acts against the colonies, charging customs duties on paint, glass, paper, and tea. The House of Burgesses again responded by asserting its authority to impose taxation on the people of Virginia, but denying Parliament that right because Virginians were not represented in Parliament. The governor of Virginia, angered by the rebellious stance, refused to allow the House to continue its meeting.

Undaunted, the burgesses went to Raleigh Tavern, near the capitol building in Williamsburg, and continued their meeting. They added a nonimportation and nonconsumption agreement to their previous statement about taxation without representation. The agreement stated that the people of Virginia would not import or purchase any goods taxed by Parliament. To show how serious they were about the issue, they even agreed to stop importing slaves after November 1, an action that, if carried out, could severely affect the economy of Virginia. But they did not have to follow through: Because of widespread opposition to the Townshend Acts, Parliament repealed the duties in 1770 on everything but tea.

By this time, middle-class Virginians were actively protesting British oppression, in particular the Quartering Act, which was imposed about the same time as the Stamp Act and forced the colonies to provide lodging, food, and other supplies for British soldiers. When the New York Legislature refused to enforce the Quartering Act, Parliament ordered the legislature to stop meeting. In protest, many Virginians signed petitions and forwarded them to the House of Burgesses. In the records of the House, it is noted that the petitions influenced the burgesses to declare that the Quartering Act and Townshend duties were "cruel and unconstitutional," and that their passage was "destructive of the Liberty of a free People."[25] Liberty and freedom were becoming rallying cries to the people of Virginia.

Realizing that further British oppression was inevitable and called for organized resistance, Virginia persuaded the other colonies to form committees of correspondence. These committees would "correspond with other legislators or their committees about activities deemed dangerous to America."[26] Within a year, all the colonies except Pennsylvania had formed committees. Virginia had led the way in influencing all the colonies to take a step toward working together for a common cause.

## Virginians React to the Boston Tea Party

Virginia showed that it was sympathetic to the causes of other colonies when patriots in Boston decided to protest the tea tax still imposed on the colonies as part of the Townshend duties. On the night of December 16, 1773, a band of colonists, some dressed as Indians, crept aboard a British ship in Boston Harbor. The ship had carried tea to America but had not been allowed to unload the tea in port. The patriots gathered up the boxes of tea and dumped them into the harbor. Dubbed "the Boston Tea Party," this rebellious act became a symbol of the patriot cause.

The Boston Tea Party became a symbol of patriotism.

In March 1774 Parliament responded to the Boston Tea Party by deciding to close the port of Boston by June. To show its sympathy to the people of Boston and its commitment to the patriot cause, the House of Burgesses declared June 7, 1774, as a "Day of Fasting, Humiliation, and Prayer, devoutly to implore the divine Interposition for averting the heavy Calamity, which threatens Destruction to our civil Rights, and the Evils of Civil War." [27] Virginia's royal governor, Lord Dunmore, responded to the day of fasting by dissolving the House, hoping that would put an end to

Lord Dunmore, Virginia's royal governor, dissolved the House of Burgesses.

its patriot sympathies. Against his orders, the House of Burgesses renamed itself the Virginia Convention, met again at Raleigh Tavern in Williamsburg, and called for a convention of the colonies.

Called the First Continental Congress, the convention of all colonies except Georgia met in Philadelphia, Pennsylvania, in September 1774. Virginia sent seven delegates: Peyton Randolph, Richard Henry Lee, George Washington, Edmund Pendleton, Patrick Henry, Richard Bland, and Benjamin Harrison. The delegates from the other colonies were impressed with the men from Virginia. John Adams wrote that they were "the most spirited and consistent, of any." And Caesar Rodney of Delaware wrote of the Virginia delegates, "more sensible, fine fellows you would never wish to see." [28]

## The Colony Prepares for War

In March 1775 British troops were gathering in Massachusetts. In reaction to this threat, the Virginia Convention met to discuss what action to take. Patrick Henry knew exactly what he thought they should do, and he told the Convention so in a famous speech. Calling on Virginians to support a war with Britain, he declared:

Patrick Henry declared, "give me liberty, or give me death!" before the Virginia Convention.

Gentleman may cry, "Peace! Peace!"—but there is no peace. The war is actually begun! The next gale that sweeps from the north will bring to our ears the clash of resounding arms! Our brethren are already in the field! Why stand we here idle? . . . Is life so dear, or peace so sweet, as to be purchased at the price of chains and slavery? Forbid it, Almighty God! I know not what course others may take; but as for me, give me liberty, or give me death! [29]

The stirring speech had its desired effect. The members of the Virginia Convention voted to go into a posture of defense and to prepare the colony's militias for war.

Governor Dunmore reacted to these proceedings by seizing gunpowder from the magazine at Williamsburg, apparently hoping to weaken the patriot cause. When the local militia heard of his actions, they marched on Williamsburg. Dunmore promised to return the powder, but he did not, so more militia, led by Patrick Henry, marched on Williamsburg. Finally, Dunmore paid for the powder.

Frightened by the presence of so many rebels, Dunmore fled the capital for a British warship in the York River. Hearing rumors that some in Virginia thought he should be hanged, Dunmore then ordered the ship to sail to Norfolk. The determined patriots of Virginia had forced out the royal governor; at this point they were in practice a truly self-governing colony.

In November 1775 Dunmore issued a proclamation declaring, in other words, that slaves and indentured servants would be granted freedom if they took up arms and fought against the Americans. In all, it is estimated that about eight hundred slaves fled their plantations and joined Dunmore.

With this action, Dunmore had sealed his fate. He was no longer welcome in Virginia; the planters had feared a slave uprising for years, and Dunmore had furthered the possibility of one, turning many who had been wavering in their support for the rebels against him. For not all of the people of Virginia were on the side of the patriot cause. However, those who remained loyal to Great Britain, called Loyalists or Tories, faced persecution if they stayed in Virginia. While the Tory presence in Virginia, along with that in New England, was the weakest of any of the colonies, there were Tory factions, and some were aggressive.

But as passions for freedom rose, some contentious Tories were hanged. In Montgomery County, for example, Tories tried to seize lead mines—musketballs were made from lead, and they did not want the Americans to be able to get the lead—and Colonel Charles Lynch, superintendent of mines, captured and hanged them. By 1779 Virginia authorities had confiscated hundreds of estates of those who were loyal to the British cause. Nearly all Loyalists, though, had already fled in 1775 and 1776, when the American Revolution began.

On May 15, 1776, the Virginia Convention met again. This time, delegates adopted a resolution to "declare the United Colonies free and independent states, absolved from all allegiance to, or dependence upon, the Crown or Parliament of Great Britain."[30] Then someone pulled down the British flag from the top of the capitol building. The people of Williamsburg gathered around the building and cheered.

## The Constitution of Virginia

Steady in its course toward independence, the Virginia Convention decided to draft a constitution for their now free state. The constitution was to include a declaration of rights, to be written by George Mason. The declaration included many of the same rights named in the American Declaration of Independence. In fact, while Mason was penning Virginia's Declaration of Rights in June 1776, Thomas Jefferson, another prominent Virginian, was just beginning to draft the Declaration of Independence. It is widely believed that Jefferson drew upon Mason's declaration when considering the content of the Declaration of Independence.

# George Mason

Patriot and statesman George Mason was born in Fairfax County in 1725. He was George Washington's neighbor and a member of the Ohio Company, formed to promote trade and settlement in the area of the Upper Ohio River. Mason also helped to found the city of Alexandria. He was elected to the House of Burgesses in 1759.

In 1776 Mason drew up Virginia's first constitution. He included a Declaration of Rights that later inspired the Declaration of Independence and the U.S. Bill of Rights. Included in Virginia's Declaration of Rights are calls for religious toleration and these words:

That all men are by nature equally free and independent, and have certain inherent rights … namely, the enjoyment of life and liberty, with the means of acquiring and possessing property, and pursuing and obtaining happiness and safety.

George Mason drew up Virginia's first constitution.

Mason spoke at the Constitutional Convention in 1787 but would not sign the Constitution because it did not contain a bill of rights. He campaigned for a bill of rights until one was added to the Constitution in 1791.

Mason lived at Gunston Hall on the Potomac River. His home still stands today.

The Virginia state constitution was approved in June 1776. Virginia declared itself an independent commonwealth, asserting that the people of Virginia have the right to make their own laws.

## A Country Comes Together

The drive for freedom had fully caught on in Virginia. At the Second Continental Congress a few weeks earlier, Virginian Richard Henry Lee, with the support of most of the Virginia delegates, introduced this motion: "That these United Colonies are, and of right ought to be, free and independent States, that they are absolved from all allegiance to the British Crown, and that all political connection between them and the State of Great Britain is, and ought to be, totally dissolved."[31] While

Richard Henry Lee moved the motion that led to the Declaration of Independence.

most Virginians were ready to accept such an idea, not everyone at the Philadelphia congress was. They decided to postpone voting on the motion until July, after the Declaration of Independence was completed.

On July 2, 1776, the Continental Congress decided to approve Lee's resolution. Then the declaration was read and discussed. On July 4, after a few minor changes, it too was approved. With the support of the Commonwealth of Virginia and the words of the Declaration of Independence, the United States was born:

That whenever any Form of Government becomes destructive of these ends, it is the Right of the People to alter or to abolish it, and to institute new Government, laying its foundation on such principles and organizing its powers in such form, as to them shall seem most likely to effect their Safety and Happiness.

As the Continental Congress approved these words, the new nation prepared to fight a war that would take many lives, but that resulted in

# The Virginia Dynasty

George Washington's grandfather, Lawrence, came to Virginia in 1657 and soon acquired thousands of acres of land. When George was a child, his family moved to Mount Vernon and built a plantation house there. As a teenager, Washington was a surveyor, but he soon moved on to military service. After distinguishing himself in the French and Indian War, as a member of the House of Burgesses, and as a delegate to the First Continental Congress, Washington was named commander of the Continental Army. With victory came celebrity and public office, something he did not always appreciate because it left him little time to farm and spend with his family. After he was elected president of the Constitutional Convention, there was little doubt he would be elected president of the country, and in 1789 he was unanimously elected the country's leader.

Washington selected two Virginians as members of his cabinet: Thomas Jefferson became secretary of state, and Edmund Randolph was chosen as attorney general. Another Virginian and friend of Washington's, James Madison,

George Washington was unanimously elected first president of the United States.

was a close advisor. Jefferson later became the third U.S. president, after John Adams of Massachusetts. Jefferson served two terms and was succeeded by James Madison, who was president from 1809 to 1817. Madison had been Jefferson's secretary of state as well as a U.S. representative and a member of the Virginia Assembly. James Monroe, born in Westmoreland County, led the country next, serving two terms as the fifth president. Thus, four of the first five presidents were Virginians, creating what is called "the Virginia Dynasty."

Men listen as the Declaration of Independence is read.

the reality of what Virginians had been working toward for so many years: freedom. Middlekauff writes that "none had contributed more to the Revolution than Virginia." He goes on to say that the gentry "led Virginia into the Revolution and continued to lead afterwards."[32] The road to independence was not an easy one; once they had achieved their goal, would those who governed Virginia be able to live up to it?

## Chapter Five

# Virginia After the Revolution

The years following the Revolution were challenging ones for Virginia, as the elite who had led the fight for freedom and democracy tried to incorporate those values into its existing society. While the gentry who had ruled Virginia for generations valued liberty and democracy, when it came to their own state they were not so quick to embrace the principles that had fueled the Revolution. The potential for freedom that resulted from the Revolution threatened the class-based way of life in Virginia, and while the ruling class adopted some very democratic measures, such as the Statute for Religious Freedom, they thwarted others dealing with personal freedom and public education.

The first draft of Virginia's Bill of Rights.

### The First Step: Virginia's Declaration of Rights

The first step toward democracy and equality had occurred in 1776, when Virginia drafted its

Declaration of Rights. George Mason, the author of the declaration, called for "tolerance" of those who were religious dissenters, but statesman James Madison persuaded the Virginia Convention to go a step further. He believed that religious freedom was a right, not something to be tolerated or conceded, writing that religion was "a matter of individual conscience and not within the cognizance of civil government." [33] Mason soon agreed with Madison, and section 16 of the declaration reflects Madison's influence, stating

Virginia's Declaration of Rights was the state's first step toward democracy.

that "all men are equally entitled to the free exercise of religion, according to the dictates of conscience." [34]

The declaration brought Virginia a step closer to democracy. The wording of section 1 of the declaration clarified this goal:

> That all men are by nature free and independent and have certain inherent rights, of which, when they enter into a state of society, they cannot, by any compact, deprive or divest their posterity; namely, the enjoyment of life and liberty, with the means of possessing property, and pursuing and obtaining happiness and safety. [35]

The wording, however, is conveniently subtle; the Virginia Convention, realizing that they could not honestly say that everyone in the state was truly free, added the phrase "when they enter into a state of society" for the purpose of excluding slaves. Slaves were not in a "state of society"; they were quartered away from society, all the while forced to help maintain that society and the lifestyle of the gentry.

Although many of the members of the convention were ideologically opposed to slavery, they were slaveowners themselves; even the most outspoken proponent of freedom and equality, Thomas Jefferson,

Thomas Jefferson, an outspoken proponent of freedom, owned slaves.

owned slaves. The only way all Virginians could be truly free, the gentry knew, was for everyone to free their slaves. But to them, this was not economically feasible, and many of them, including Jefferson, even believed that freeing slaves would be unfair to the slaves themselves. Jefferson wrote that if slaves were freed, they should be given a separate colony to live in, because

deep rooted prejudiced entertained by the whites; ten thousand recollections, by the blacks, of the injuries they have sustained; new provocations; the real distinctions which nature has made; and many other circumstances, will divide into parties, and produce convulsions which will probably never end but in the extermination of the one or the other race. [36]

So, though Virginia's elites had fought for equality and democracy, in the end they failed to provide it for everyone in their own state. After the Revolution, slaves still could be bought and sold; they could not leave their masters' plantations without permission, nor could they testify in a court case involving a white person. Although in 1787 slavery was prohibited in the new states being formed from the Northwest Territory, including Ohio, Indiana, Illinois, Michigan, and Wisconsin, the institution was still legal—and still considered an economic necessity—in Virginia. And when George Mason called for the abolition of slavery on a national level at the Constitutional Convention in May 1787, most of the states disagreed, postponing a decision on the issue until 1808.

## The Statute for Religious Freedom

To many in Virginia after the Revolution, the most important issue was religious freedom. For years, the Anglican Church was the established, or state, church in Virginia, and a percentage of the taxes collected from the citizens of Virginia was given to the church. For years, few complained about this lack of separation of church and state. The gentry and yeomen worshiped in Anglican churches throughout the colony, secure in the notion that their neighbors, at least outwardly, believed as they did.

But as the colony grew, a more diverse group of people arrived. In the early and mid–eighteenth century, many Scotch-Irish immigrants were adherents of other religious denominations, primarily Presbyterian and Baptist. Virginia law allowed them to declare themselves dissenters so that they could be exempt from paying taxes to the Anglican Church. But even while they dissented, some of the

Slavery was considered an economic necessity in colonial Virginia.

general taxes they paid went to the church anyway; a certain percentage went to the upkeep of church buildings, and Anglican vestries levied taxes to help the poor.

The Baptists and Presbyterians protested this policy. They wanted complete freedom to worship as they pleased, and they did not want to contribute financially to a church that was not their own. They protested against other inequities as well. One point of contention was the license that "foreign" congregations had to obtain before they could gather and worship—Virginia required Presbyterian and Baptist ministers to register all the places they expected to preach with the county court, which would then issue them a license. The new denominations, particularly the Separate Baptists, felt that this requirement did not allow them to worship freely. Separate Baptist ministers felt oppressed by the Anglican Church and were quick to criticize it from the pulpit. The Separate Baptists were popular in the Piedmont and Tidewater regions, and their noisy, jubilant worship services offended the more staid Anglicans.

When members of local government (all of whom, of course, were Anglicans) discovered that many Baptist ministers were not registering

The Anglican Church was supported by state taxes.

# John Marshall

John Marshall was the fourth chief justice of the U.S. Supreme Court and an important figure in American law. He served on the Court for thirty-four years, longer than any other chief justice to date.

Marshall was born in 1755 in Germantown, Virginia. His father was a member of the House of Burgesses and a county sheriff. Marshall was a member of the Continental Army during the Revolution and served with George Washington's forces at Valley Forge in the winter of 1777–1778. After the war, he studied law at the College of William and Mary for only six weeks, then was admitted to the Virginia bar.

John Marshall served thirty-four years as Chief Justice of the Supreme Court.

In 1782 Marshall was elected to the Virginia legislature. He was a delegate to the Virginia Convention to determine whether to ratify the U.S. Constitution. In 1797 Marshall became U.S. minister to France. In 1799 he was elected to the U.S. House of Representatives, and in 1800 President John Adams named him secretary of state. Adams then named him chief justice in 1801.

As chief justice, Marshall helped define the role of the Supreme Court in American government. Virginius Dabney, in the book *Virginia: The New Dominion* calls him a "legal genius," saying that Marshall "helped to transform a handful of weak and quarreling states into a united nation." Marshall and Thomas Jefferson were cousins, but the two did not get along. Jefferson vehemently believed in equality, while Marshall did not trust rule by "the people."

their services and did not have licenses, they arrested and jailed about thirty-four of them. Other Anglicans reacted to the Baptists by forming mobs and attacking them. According to Virginius Dabney, Baptists were "plunged into mud until they were nearly drowned, out of ridicule of the Baptist rite of dipping"[37] ("dipping" refers to the Baptist form of baptism by immersing the entire body in water).

In 1775 the Hanover Presbytery filed a petition with the legislature asking for laws that would allow them complete freedom of worship, with no ties to the established church. This petition brought the issue of religious freedom to the forefront. Although the Virginia Declaration of Rights, passed in 1776, stated that Virginians were entitled to the free exercise of religion, the dissenting congregations continued to feel oppressed by the requirement to register and obtain licenses and by the tax monies they involuntarily contributed to Anglican causes.

The Methodists, a Protestant denomination that had broken away from the Anglican Church in 1776, also became dissenters. As a separate denomination, they joined the Baptists and Presbyterians in calling for religious freedom. The three denominations were supporters of political freedom as well, and their contributions and sacrifices to the cause of freedom during the Revolution could not be ignored.

From 1775 to 1783 the issue of religious freedom had been eclipsed by the struggle for independence from Great Britain. But after the Revolution the issue was again at the forefront. As early as 1779, then Governor Thomas Jefferson had drafted and introduced the Statute for Religious Freedom, which did not pass. In 1786, while Jefferson was the American ambassador to France, he and his good friend James Madison decided conditions were right to reintroduce the bill. That same year, Madison presented the statute to Virginia's legislature. The statute passed by a vote of 74 to 20.

The statute contains this paragraph:

> *Be it enacted by the General Assembly,* That no man shall be compelled to frequent or support any religious worship, place, or ministry whatsoever, nor shall be enforced, restrained, molested or burthened [burdened] in his body or

goods, nor shall otherwise suffer on account of his religious opinions or belief; but that all men shall be free to profess, and by argument to maintain, their opinions in matters of religion, and that the same shall in no wise diminish, enlarge or affect their civil capacities. [38]

The passage of the bill showed that Virginia's ruling class was at last ready to concede that the days of an established church were over; in doing so, the gentry was also conceding to the cause of freedom an element of its tradition and lifestyle that had endured for generations. The statute disestablished the Anglican Church (soon to be called the

# James Madison

James Madison is known as the "Father of the Constitution." His first role in government was member of the Committee of Safety in Orange County. In 1776 he helped to write the first Virginia Constitution and the Declaration of Rights.

In 1778, Madison became a member of the governor's council. A year later he was elected to the Continental Congress. Madison became a member of the U.S. House of Representatives in 1789, where he was primarily responsible for drafting the first ten amendments, or Bill of Rights, to the Constitution, and he led the fight for its adoption in 1791. He is also responsible for writing twenty-nine of the letters included in the *Federalist*, a series of papers published anonymously in newspapers in 1787 and 1788 encouraging ratification of the U.S. Constitution and later collected as a set. At the Constitutional Convention in 1787 he distinguished himself by his vast knowledge of politics and historical documents. He also acted as secretary and provided a clear, comprehensive record of its proceedings.

When Thomas Jefferson became president in 1801, he named Madison as his secretary of state. When Jefferson's second term ended, Madison became president. In response to trade problems with Britain and France, Madison and Congress declared war on Great Britain in 1812. In 1814, British soldiers attacked the city of Washington, D.C., and burned the White House, and Madison and his wife, Dolley, had to flee. The war ended in 1815.

Episcopal Church). Once a powerful symbol in Virginia, the Anglican Church lost much of its power. By 1790 other denominations had converted about thirty-seven thousand members, or about 25 percent of all the families in Virginia.

After the passage of the statute, many Virginians petitioned the government to sell off the properties belonging to the Anglican Church and to give the proceeds to the poor. In 1799 the General Assembly repealed earlier legislation that had reserved to the church all of its property, and in 1802 the assembly directed that the land be sold. Some of the proceeds did go to the poor, but other monies went to the support of private schools or even to unscrupulous politicians.

Thomas Jefferson, the author of the Statute for Religious Freedom, had also drafted another bill that would weaken the hold of the aristocracy on his beloved Virginia by outlawing primogeniture in the state. It remained to be seen whether the leaders of Virginia were ready to ban such a long-held tradition.

## Jefferson's Bill Against Primogeniture

The bill outlawed primogeniture, an accepted right of the eldest son to inherit all of his father's property if his father died without a will. In 1776 the assembly had passed a related law introduced by Jefferson dealing with entail, which is the passage of property through a particular family line, without exception, save for a special act of legislation. These practices were remnants of the British legal code, and Jefferson saw no place for them in a democracy, as they perpetuated the idea of a privileged elite. The bill against primogeniture passed in 1786; with its passage, the General Assembly at least acknowledged the idea that there was no place for an aristocracy in their new and democratic state.

But Jefferson was intent on addressing yet another vital issue: education.

## Jefferson's Education Bill

In 1786 Thomas Jefferson presented a bill that would guarantee public education to all children in Virginia. While he believed that only the most intelligent should govern, he also believed that men of ability could be found anywhere, not just in the gentry class. The bill, called "A Bill for the More General Diffusion of Knowledge," proposed that schools for both girls and boys be established at public expense. The three-year schools would teach a basic curriculum, while publicly funded schools of higher learning, or grammar schools, would teach Latin, Greek, English, geography, and difficult arithmetic. Parents who could afford to do so would pay to send their children to the schools, but poor children would be welcome as well, their tuition paid by public funds. Jefferson's bill also proposed that the most

Thomas Jefferson drafted several bills to promote social equality.

promising senior among Virginia's poor students would be given a scholarship to the College of William and Mary, in Williamsburg.

The assembly voted down the bill, citing the heavy financial burdens it would place on citizens and the difficulty of administrating such a plan. But historian Robert Middlekauff states that an underlying reason the bill did not pass was that "it may have seemed to promise more social equality than most Virginia planters wanted." [39] The idea that the talent to govern could be found in the poor as well as the rich—in persons who, while talented, were not of the upper class—may have been too radical to accept. Virginius Dabney writes that "leading citizens often were lacking in enthusiasm for the establishment of public education for the less affluent, especially if it meant in increase in taxes." [40] Their children were being educated at private academies, and they were not concerned about the children of poor families. As a result, there was no statewide system of public education in Virginia for poor children—those whose parents could not afford to send them to private academies—until after the Civil War. The General Assembly did establish a Literary Fund in 1810 to encourage learning, and in 1811 it passed "An Act to Provide for the Education of the Poor," but overall the general education of the children of Virginia was overlooked.

Their position on education illustrated the ambivalence of the leaders of Virginia about sacrificing the traditions of the past for the realities of the present. They were committed to the principles of democracy and freedom, but they were not yet willing to give up the way of life that had, for them, worked so well. Charles F. Hobson explains the beliefs of the aristocracy this way:

> They sincerely believed in "popular" government in the sense of a fairly widespread voting franchise (among white males owning at least some property) but that government itself would continue to be the preserve of the "better sort," gentlemen of sufficient property, education, and leisure to enable them to govern wisely and virtuously.[41]

Some of the state's "old guard" even feared that ratification of the federal Constitution would result in the demise of the old ways. Virginia's governor, Benjamin Harrison, signer of the Declaration of Independence and father and great-grandfather of future presidents, was a member of the ruling elite. Fearful of losing the way of life he

Though they were committed to the idea of democracy and freedom, some statesmen feared that the Constitution would mean sacrificing tradition.

held so dear, he wrote to George Mason, "If the constitution is carried into effect, the states south of the Potomac will be little more than appendages to those northward of it."[42] But Virginia was on a course toward democracy. It would take until 1830 for persons other than white landowners to be given the right to vote, and, with the rest of the South, until much later for slaves to gain their freedom. But eventually Virginia again became a place of opportunity for those pursuing the American dream, much the way it had been back in 1607.

# Notes

## Chapter One: The First Colony

1. "The First Charter of Virginia; April 10, 1606," The Avalon Project at the Yale Law School, www.yale.edu/lawweb/avalon/states/va 01.htm.
2. Quoted in David Freeman Hawke, ed., *Captain John Smith's History of Virginia*. New York: Bobbs-Merrill, 1970, p. 27.
3. Quoted in Hawke, *Captain John Smith's History*, p. 42.
4. Quoted in Hawke, *Captain John Smith's History*, p. 118.

## Chapter Two: The Colony Grows

5. Quoted in "John Rolfe," Association for the Preservation of Antiquities, www.apva.org/history/jrolfe.html.
6. Quoted in Virginius Dabney, *Virginia: The New Dominion*. Garden City, NY: Doubleday, 1971, p. 71.
7. Quoted in T. H. Breen, *Tobacco Culture: The Mentality of the Great Tidewater Planters on the Eve of Revolution*. Princeton, NJ: Princeton University Press, 1985, p. 169.
8. Quoted in Breen, *Tobacco Culture*, p. 169.
9. Quoted in Breen, *Tobacco Culture*, p. 176.
10. Quoted in Breen, *Tobacco Culture*, p. 177.
11. Quoted in Breen, *Tobacco Culture*, p. 178.

## Chapter Three: Daily Life in Colonial Virginia

12. Quoted in David Allan Williams, "The Small Farmer in Eighteenth-Century Virginia Politics," in Stanley N. Katz and John M. Murrin, eds., *Colonial America: Essays in Politics and Social Development*. New York: Knopf, 1983, p. 414.
13. Quoted in Clifford Dowdey, *The Great Plantation: A Profile of Berkeley Hundred and Plantation from Jamestown to Appomattox*. New York: Bonanza, 1957, p. 154.
14. Quoted in Allan Kulikoff, *Tobacco & Slaves: The Development of Southern Cultures in the Chesapeake, 1680–1800*. Chapel Hill: University of North Carolina Press, 1986, p. 218.

15. Quoted in Kulikoff, *Tobacco & Slaves*, p. 218.
16. Quoted in Benson Bobrick, *Angel in the Whirlwind: The Triumph of the American Revolution*. New York: Simon & Schuster, 1997, p. 39.
17. Quoted in Dabney, *Virginia*, p. 40.
18. Quoted in Susie M. Ames, *Reading, Writing, and Arithmetic in Virginia, 1607–1699*. Williamsburg: Virginia 350th Anniversary Celebration Corporation, 1957, p. 19.
19. Quoted in Ames, *Reading, Writing, and Arithmetic*, p. 9.

## Chapter Four: Virginia's Role in the American Revolution

20. Quoted in Robert Middlekauff, *The Glorious Cause: The American Revolution, 1763–1789*. New York: Oxford University Press, 1982, p. 81.
21. Quoted in Middlekauff, *Glorious Cause*, p. 82.
22. Quoted in Middlekauff, *Glorious Cause*, p. 82.
23. Quoted in Middlekauff, *Glorious Cause*, p. 126.
24. Middlekauff, *Glorious Cause*, p. 137.
25. Quoted in Middlekauff, *Glorious Cause*, p. 179.
26. Middlekauff, *Glorious Cause*, p. 215.
27. Quoted in Middlekauff, *Glorious Cause*, p. 233.
28. Quoted in Middlekauff, *Glorious Cause*, p. 241.
29. Patrick Henry, "Liberty or Death!" The History Place Great Speeches Collection, www.historyplace.com/speeches/henry.htm.
30. Quoted in Dabney, *Virginia*, p. 135.
31. Quoted in Middlekauff, *Glorious Cause*, p. 325.
32. Middlekauff, *Glorious Cause*, p. 605.

## Chapter Five: Virginia After the Revolution

33. Quoted in Daniel L. Dreisbach, "George Mason's Pursuit of Religious Liberty in Revolutionary Virginia," *Virginia Magazine of History and Biography*, vol. 108, no. 1 (2000), p. 35.
34. "The Virginia Declaration of Rights," National Archives and Records Administration/www.nara.gov/exhall/charters/bill rights/virginia.html.
35. "The Virginia Declaration of Rights," http://www.nara.gov/exhall/charters/billrights/virginia.html.
36. Quoted in Middlekauff, *Glorious Cause*, p. 612.
37. Dabney, *Virginia*, p. 161.
38. Quoted in Dabney, *Virginia*, p. 163.

39. Middlekauff, *Glorious Cause*, p. 613.
40. Dabney, *Virginia*, p. 245.
41. Charles F. Hobson, *The Great Chief Justice: John Marshall and the Rule of Law.* Lawrence: University Press of Kansas, 1996, p. ix.
42. Quoted in Dowdey, *The Great Plantation*, p. 284.

# Chronology

**1607**
Jamestown is founded in May.

**1612**
John Rolfe harvests his first tobacco crop in Jamestown.

**1618**
Headright system instituted in Virginia.

**1619**
First General Assembly meets in Jamestown; first slaves arrive in Virginia.

**1622**
Indian massacre of 349 settlers near Jamestown.

**1624**
Virginia Company of London dissolves; Virginia becomes a royal colony.

**1660**
Navigation Act enforced.

**1661**
Virginia General Assembly legalizes slavery.

**1676**
Bacon's Rebellion.

**1693**
College of William and Mary receives charter.

**1699**
Williamsburg becomes capital of Virginia.

**1730**
House of Burgesses passes the Virginia Tobacco Act.

**1774**
House of Burgesses declares day of sympathy for Boston Tea Party; Governor Dunmore dissolves House of Burgesses; House renames itself the Virginia Convention and meets at Raleigh Tavern; First Continental Congress meets in Philadelphia; Virginia sends eight delegates; Virginian Randolph Peyton named president of Congress.

**1775**
In March, Virginia Convention takes posture of defense against British; Patrick Henry delivers "Liberty or Death" speech; in May, Dunmore flees Williamsburg and Second Continental Congress convenes; George Washington named to lead Continental Army; in November, Dunmore declares martial law and issues emancipation proclamation.

**1776**
In June, Virginia adopts new state constitution and Declaration of Rights; Thomas Jefferson named to write Declaration of Independence; Declaration of Independence adopted July 4.

**1778**
In July, Virginia votes to ratify Articles of Confederation.

**1779**
Richmond becomes new capital of Virginia.

**1786**
Statute for Religious Freedom passes in Virginia.

**1787**
Constitutional Convention.

**1788**
Virginia ratifies U.S. Constitution and becomes tenth state.

# For Further Reading

Bruce Bliven Jr., *The American Revolution*. New York: Random House, 1958. An easy-to-read account of the major events in the Revolutionary War.

Natalie S. Bober, *Thomas Jefferson: Man on a Mountain*. New York: Aladdin, 1997. Intended for young adults, this portrait of Jefferson portrays him as a fascinating man who in many ways was ahead of his time.

Jean Fritz, *The Double Life of Pocahontas*. New York: Viking Press, 1987. This young adult book presents an accurate picture of the life of this famous Indian woman.

Joy Hakim, *From Colonies to Country: 1710–1791*. New York: Oxford University Press, 1999. Includes text, drawings, and maps that explain colonial history, including the French and Indian War, the Declaration of Independence, the Revolutionary War, and the Constitutional Convention.

———, *Making Thirteen Colonies: 1600–1740*. New York: Oxford University Press, 1999. Describes the different people who settled in America, where they came from, where they settled, and how Native Americans reacted to them.

Ivor Noel Hume, *Martin's Hundred*. Charlottesville: University Press of Virginia, 1982. A detailed account of the archaeological excavation of the seventeenth-century settlements at Martin's Hundred and Carter's Grove Plantation in Virginia.

Julius Lester, *To Be a Slave*. New York: Dial, 1998. Firsthand narratives from former slaves make this a powerful depiction of slave life in America.

John M. Rosenburg, *First in War: George Washington in the American Revolution*. Brookfield, CT: Millbrook Press, 1998. Geared toward young adults, this book describes the important role George Washington played in founding the United States.

# Works Consulted

## Books

Susie M. Ames, *Reading, Writing, and Arithmetic in Virginia, 1607–1699*. Williamsburg: Virginia 350th Anniversary Celebration Corporation, 1957. This booklet describes in detail the system of education in Virginia in the seventeenth century.

Benson Bobrick, *Angel in the Whirlwind: The Triumph of the American Revolution*. New York: Simon & Schuster, 1997. A concise, clear review of the American Revolution.

T. H. Breen, *Tobacco Culture: The Mentality of the Great Tidewater Planters on the Eve of Revolution*. Princeton, NJ: Princeton University Press, 1985. Breen's book is valuable in that it is one of few studies of the culture that emerged around the cultivation of tobacco.

Virginius Dabney, *Virginia: The New Dominion*. Garden City, NY: Doubleday, 1971. A comprehensive yet concise review of the important events in Virginia's history.

Clifford Dowdey, *The Great Plantation: A Profile of Berkeley Hundred and Plantation from Jamestown to Appomattox*. New York: Bonanza, 1957. While concentrating on one plantation, Dowdey gives a broad portrayal of plantation life and life in general in colonial Tidewater Virginia.

David Freeman Hawke, ed., *Captain John Smith's History of Virginia*. New York: Bobbs-Merrill, 1970.

Charles F. Hobson, *The Great Chief Justice: John Marshall and the Rule of Law*. Lawrence: University Press of Kansas, 1996. Geared toward those who are interested in Marshall's place in the history of American jurisprudence.

Allan Kulikoff, *Tobacco & Slaves: The Development of Southern Cultures in the Chesapeake, 1680–1800*. Chapel Hill: University of North Carolina Press, 1986. A highly detailed explanation of every facet of the formation of the Chesapeake colonies of Virginia and Maryland. Many tables and statistics make this an invaluable resource in the study of colonial settlement.

Robert Middlekauff, *The Glorious Cause: The American Revolution, 1763–1789*. New York: Oxford University Press, 1982. Traces the movements in the colonies that led to the Revolution and highlights the contributions of each colony to the cause of independence.

Helen Rountree, *Pocahontas's People: The Powhatan Indians of Virginia Through Four Centuries*. Norman: University of Oklahoma Press, 1996. A title in the Civilization of the American Indian Series. Rountree explains in detail the culture and history of the Powhatan Indians.

Arthur M. Schlesinger, *The Birth of the Nation: A Portrait of the American People on the Eve of Independence*. New York: Knopf, 1968. Schlesinger explains how the ideas of the colonists before the Revolution had come to be distinctively American, and how the people of the United States created a separate American society.

Alden Vaughan, *American Genesis: Captain John Smith and the Founding of Virginia*. Boston: Little, Brown, 1975. This book is a must-read for anyone interested in the settling of Jamestown and Captain John Smith.

David Allan Williams, "The Small Farmer in Eighteenth-Century Virginia Politics," in Stanley N. Katz and John M. Murrin, eds., *Colonial America: Essays in Politics and Social Development*. New York: Knopf, 1983.

Stephanie Wolf, *As Various as Their Land: The Everyday Lives of Eighteenth-Century Americans*. New York: HarperCollins, 1993. A fascinating picture of life in early America.

Louis B. Wright, *The Atlantic Frontier: Colonial American Civilization [1607–1763]*. Ithaca, NY: Cornell University Press, 1947. Wright describes the settlement and way of life of those who founded America.

**Periodicals**

Daniel L. Dreisbach, "George Mason's Pursuit of Religious Liberty in Revolutionary Virginia," *Virginia Magazine of History and Biography*, vol. 108, no. 1 (2000).

Woody Holton, "Rebel Against Rebel: Enslaved Virginians and the Coming of the American Revolution," *Virginia Magazine of History and Biography*, Spring 1997.

**Internet Sources**

"The First Charter of Virginia; April 10, 1606," The Avalon Project at the Yale Law School, www.yale.edu/lawweb/avalon/states/va01.htm. This site lists all of the charters relating to colonial Virginia.

Patrick Henry, "Liberty or Death!" The History Place Great Speeches Collection, www.historyplace.com/speeches/henry.htm.

Colonel H. L. Landers, F.A. *The Virginia Campaign and the Blockage and Siege of Yorktown, 1781.* Washington: U.S. Government Printing Office, 1931, www.army.mil/cmh~pg/books/RevWar/Yorktown/AWC-Ytn-fm. htm.

"The Virginia Declaration of Rights," National Archives and Records Administration, www.nara.gov/exhall/charters/billrights/virginia.html.

"John Rolfe," Association for the Preservation of Antiquities, www.apva. org/history/jrolfe.html.

"Virginia's Indian Tribes: The Powhatan Confederacy," Internet School Library Media Center, http://falcon.jmu.edu/~ramseyil/vaindians powhatan.htm. Excellent website providing a vast array of links to many Native American tribes in Virginia.

# Index

# Index

# Picture Credits

Cover photo: Hulton Getty/Archive Photos

Archive Photos, 17, 30, 43, 62

© Bettmann/CORBIS, 66, 67

© Nancy Carter/North Wind Picture Archives, 28, 29, 50

Dover Publications, Inc., 55, 65

Hulton Getty/Archive Photos, 16, 18, 19, 24, 27, 47, 58, 63

John Grafton, *The American Revolution*, Dover Publications, Inc., 1975, 75

Library of Congress, 9, 14, 53, 56, 60, 64, 68, 69, 71, 76

North Wind Picture Archives, 12, 13, 15, 21, 22, 23, 26, 32, 34, 35, 37, 39, 41, 42, 45, 49, 59, 70

Stock Montage, 48

# About the Author

Karen Price Hossell is the author of fifteen children's books and several magazine articles. She has been an editor for nearly twenty years and is also a part-time college English instructor. She lives in Winter Park, Florida, with her husband, David, and their three dogs and one cat.